Language: English

These materials are designed to assist you in learning about Hope. They should not be used for medical advice, counseling, or other health-related services. iFred, The Shine Hope Company and Kathryn Goetzke do not endorse or provide any medical advice, diagnosis, or treatment. The information provided herein should not be used for the diagnosis or treatment of any medical condition and cannot be substituted for the advice of physicians, licensed professionals, or therapists who are familiar with your specific situation. Consult a licensed medical professional, or call 911, if you are in need of immediate assistance.

ISBN: 978-1-954531-21-5

© 2024, Kathryn Goetzke

TABLE OF CONTENTS

Introduction to Hopeful Mindsets® for Veterans 4

Veteran Resources/Disclaimer 5

Guidelines for Clergy to Support Veterans 5

An Introduction to Hope and Hopelessness 7

Group Facilitation Tips 12

Setting Expectations for the Group 13

Steps to Effective Listening 14

Setting Ground Rules 15

Icebreakers and Pre-module Activities 16

Module 1: Introduction to Hope Science and Shine Hope™ 17

Module 2: Antithesis of Hope: Hopelessness 19

Module 3: Stress Skills 22

Module 4: Happiness Habits 24

Module 5: Inspired Actions 26

Module 6: Nourishing Networks 28

Module 7: Eliminating Challenges 31

Module 8: Creating a Future Using Hope 34

INTRODUCTION TO
HOPEFUL MINDSETS® FOR VETERANS

Hopeful Mindsets is based on the work of leading experts on Hope, Mindset, Mental Health, Stress, Positive Psychology, Business, Communications, and more. Using the Five Keys to **Shine Hope** as a foundation, Hopeful Mindsets introduces critical Hope skills to help anyone navigate challenges proactively with evidence-based skills. As veterans have a significant number of challenges, especially when transitioning from military to civilian life, it is a population that needs to flex Hope muscles more than most.

Hope is built through practice and repetition, just like a muscle. This program provides an opportunity to gain hands-on experience applying Hope skills to a personal challenge in a group format to normalize the conversation around hopelessness and build Hope.

Life inevitably forces us to navigate many challenges. Hopeful Mindsets is a guide to working through and overcoming those challenges through learning 'how' to Hope. Using the Hopeful Mindsets framework reduces the likelihood of challenges leading to addiction, clinical anxiety, or depression, and helps build skills to navigate PTSD and trauma in healthy ways.

This program is designed to teach Hope as a tangible skill that can be built, measured, and maintained throughout life. We aim to ensure that all people know 'how' to Hope and have the tools and resources to manage their challenges and grow Hope proactively.

VETERAN RESOURCES/DISCLAIMER

When leading a Hope-building curriculum, it's essential to remember that some veterans may experience strong or potentially triggering emotions. Topics related to Hope, mental health, and self-reflection can sometimes evoke distress, especially in individuals with past trauma or significant life experiences.

GUIDELINES FOR CLERGY TO SUPPORT VETERANS:

1. Recognize Signs of Distress: Watch for signs of discomfort, such as withdrawal, agitation, changes in tone, or visible tension. Veterans may also become silent or disengage if a topic feels distressing.

2. Provide a Safe Space: Emphasize that all feelings are valid, and let participants know they can step outside or take a break if needed. Reassure them that their well-being is the priority.

3. Acknowledge Emotions Without Judgment: If someone appears visibly affected, gently acknowledge their experience without pressing them to share details. Say something like, "It's okay if certain parts of this conversation are challenging. Take whatever time or space you need."

4. Encourage Stress Skills: Offer calming strategies that can help individuals stay grounded, such as deep breathing, focusing on their surroundings, or using a soothing object. Simple grounding exercises can help veterans feel more present and in control.

5. Know When to Pause: If a topic is especially distressing, consider pausing the session and allowing participants to regroup. It may also help to redirect focus toward lighter material before revisiting deeper themes.

6. Have Mental Health Resources Ready: Make a list of mental health resources, such as those provided below. Encourage individuals to connect with a mental health provider or peer support if they need additional help processing emotions that arise.

RESOURCES

If someone is in crisis, you can **text HOME to 741741** for immediate assistance.

Check out this directory for validated resources that help support the recovery, rehabilitation, and reintegration of veterans and their families. *(www.nrd.gov)*

If you need help finding work following your service, this resource may be of help as well. *(www.careeronestop.org/ResourcesFor/ Veteran/veteran.aspx)*

For more resources for veterans, visit *www.theshinehopecompany.com/veterans-resources/*

Check out these episodes of The Hope Matrix podcast to learn how others have overcome challenges such as traumatic brain injury, grief, deployment and transition, and homelessness.

- **Episode 19: From Heroin Addiction and Homelessness to Hope, featuring Grant Denton of The Karma Box Project** - *www.thehopematrix.com/2022/02/02/from-heroin-addiction-and-homelessness-to-Hope-featuring-grant-denton-of-the-karma-box-project/*
- **Episode 29: Embracing Grief to Find Hope, featuring Leslie Weirich** - *www.thehopematrix.com/2024/05/28/embracing-grief-to-find-Hope-featuring-leslie-weirich/*
- **Episode 27: Finding Belief, Purpose, and Hope after a Traumatic Brain Injury, featuring Damian Wąsowicz** - *www.thehopematrix.com/2024/05/13/finding-belief-purpose-and-Hope-after-a-traumatic-brain-injury-featuring-damian-wasowicz/*
- **Episode 32: Finding Hope After Active Military Duty, featuring MaCherie Dunbar** - *www.thehopematrix.com/2024/07/05/finding-Hope-after-active-military-duty-featuring-macherie-dunbar/*
- **Being Intentional in Navigating Hope as a Veteran and Civilian, featuring Thomas Harris** - *https://thehopematrix.com/2024/07/05/being-intentional-in-navigating-Hope-as-a-veteran-and-civilian-featuring-thomas-harris/*

AN INTRODUCTION TO HOPE AND HOPELESSNESS

Before you can facilitate a group on Hope, it is important to understand what it is and why it's important. Hope is a vision for something in the future, fueled both by positive feelings and inspired actions. This definition was developed by our founder, Kathryn Goetzke, after doctors told her she was at a high risk of suicide. Her determination to get to the root cause of suicide (hopelessness) has led her to create programming to teach Hope to populations across the world. Hope is measurable, teachable, and predictive of many positive outcomes. It is specifically relevant to veteran populations because of their unique challenges to Hope both during deployment and after they return home. Transitioning to civilian life requires navigating different responsibilities and social situations with people who may not understand life in the military. Re-entering the job market, old social groups and relationships, and building a new community after coming home require special attention to a Hopeful Mindset.

We are not taught how to identify or manage hopelessness, which commonly arises in periods of challenging transition. **Hopelessness** is the combination of *emotional despair (anger, sadness, or fear)* and *motivational helplessness (a sense of powerlessness)*. We have all experienced this combination at some point, but moments of hopelessness are especially common for veterans. Left unmanaged, hopelessness can lead to adverse outcomes like violence, addiction, depression, chronic disease, anxiety, suicide, and poor health.

In this program, we acknowledge that it is impossible to avoid moments of hopelessness entirely, and instead explore techniques to manage these moments and build our capacity for Hope. Our modules cover practices such as Happiness Habits and Stress Skills that help us move from feelings of helplessness to action, supplementing and explaining the intuitive skills that individuals may already be using to navigate hopelessness in healthy ways. We will also explore the biological bases of hopelessness, equipping veterans with the scientific knowledge behind some of their behaviors and experiences. It can be confusing to understand the momentary emotional 'boost' that comes from violence and addiction when these actions inevitably result in negative outcomes, and learning alternative methods to release happiness hormones that don't have adverse effects is empowering. The science-based dialogue that this program opens up helps veterans access a network of support to learn positive, healthy coping mechanisms for challenges they face.

HOPE is a vision for something in your future, fueled by both **POSITIVE FEELINGS** and **INSPIRED ACTIONS.**

Higher Hope is associated with reduced likelihood of anxiety and depression, less likelihood of risky behaviors and addiction, less loneliness, and better quality relationships. It is linked to higher grades, improved attention in class, and less likelihood of weapon carrying in school.

Specifically relevant to veterans, higher Hope is associated with greater life satisfaction and increased efficacy of psychotherapy treatment for postt-raumatic stress disorder and depression, homelessness prevention and breaking the cycle of poverty. Additionally, and most importantly, Hope is linked to the prevention of suicidal ideation and suicide attempts.

Hope is a learnable, measurable, and teachable skill. Every person can use skills to create, maintain, and grow Hope. We teach the critical Hope skills using the Five Keys to SHINE Hope:

Stress Skills
Happiness Habits
Inspired Actions
Nourishing Networks
Eliminating Challenges

THE
HOPE MATRIX™

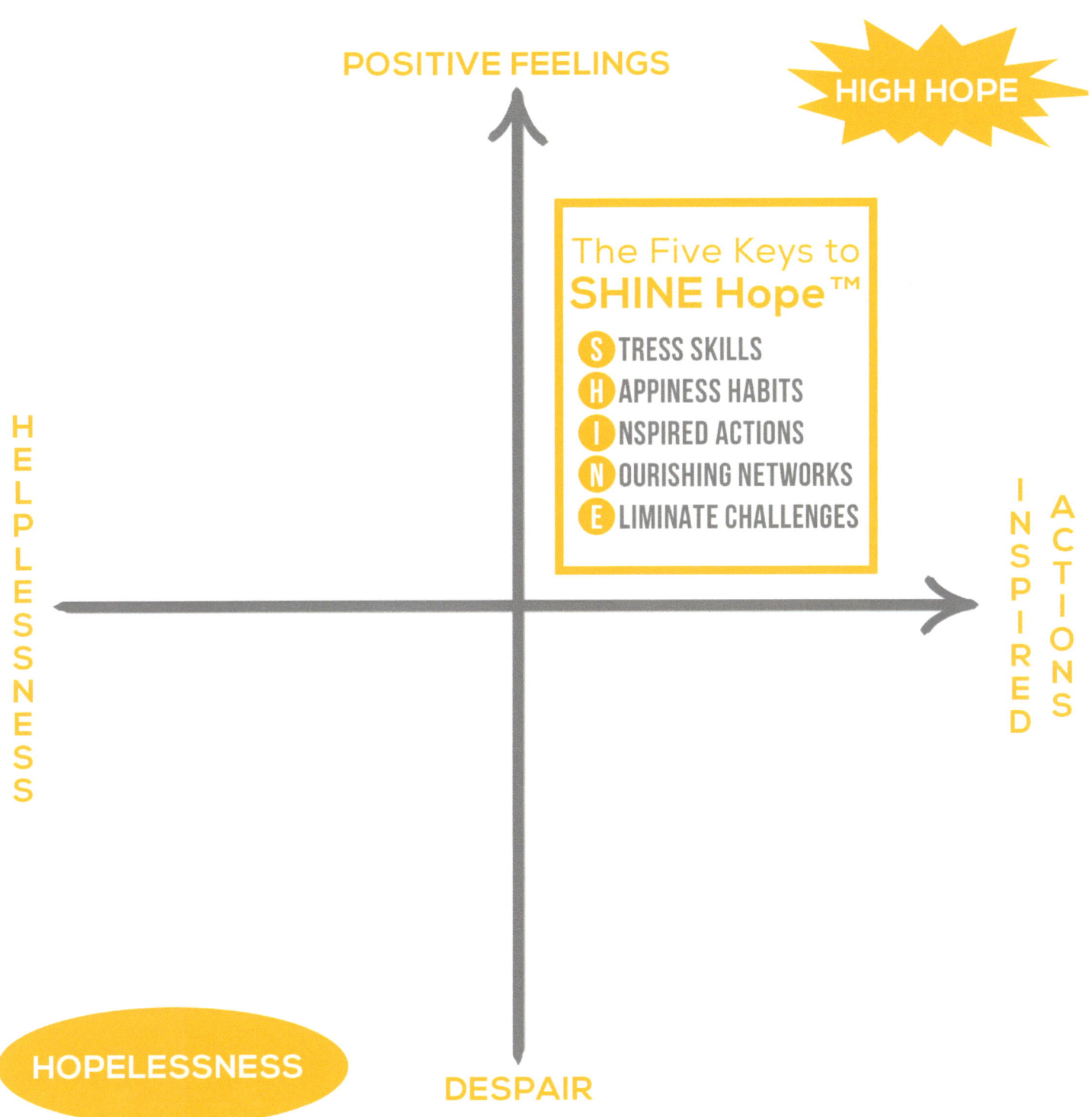

POSITIVE FEELINGS

HIGH HOPE

The Five Keys to
SHINE Hope™
- **S** TRESS SKILLS
- **H** APPINESS HABITS
- **I** NSPIRED ACTIONS
- **N** OURISHING NETWORKS
- **E** LIMINATE CHALLENGES

HELPLESSNESS

INSPIRED ACTIONS

HOPELESSNESS

DESPAIR

SHINE HOPE™
A HOW-TO FOR HOPE IN TRYING TIMES

Scan to download the clickable version of this infographic

STRESS SKILLS	**H**APPINESS HABITS	**I**NSPIRED ACTIONS	**N**OURISHING NETWORKS	**E**LIMINATING CHALLENGES
90 second pause	Activating purpose	WOOP process	5:1 Rule	Limiting beliefs
Belly breathing	Pursuing passion	SMART goals	Compassion	Automatic Negative Thoughts (ANTs)
Journaling	Utilizing strengths	Stretch goals	Forgiveness	All-or-nothing thinking
Gardening	Meditation	Achievement goals	Love	Negative bias
Calming music	Smiling	Intrinsic goals	Gratitude	Rumination & Worry
Affirming beliefs	Exercising / Nutrition	Mastery goals	Recognition	Focusing on Uncontrollables
Sensory engagement	Creating / listening to music	Micro goals / Stepping	Support	Attaching to outcomes
Cold plunge	Dancing / Singing	Habit Stacking	Faith	Internalizing failure
Decluttering	Drawing / Painting	Visualization	Trust	Toxic Consumption
Prayer	Gratitude	Overcoming obstacles	Respect	Nocebo Effect
Nature walk	Volunteering	Regoaling	Effective Listening	Mind Wandering
Napping	Wonder / Awe	Write down goals / check in	Empathy	Implicit Bias
Laughter	Quality sleep		Kindness	Negative Framing
Crying	Doodling		Animals	Perfectionism
Tapping				Taking things personally
Yoga				
Mantras				

the **shine hope**™ company

© The Shine Hope Company, LLC

Scan the QR Code to measure hope with the Hope Scale!

As you learn the Five Keys to **Shine Hope™**, there are several terms to remember, including:

HOPE: We define Hope as a vision for something in the future, fueled by both positive feelings and inspired actions.

HOPELESSNESS: Hopelessness is a feeling of despair and a sense of helplessness. It is both emotional (a negative feeling) and motivational (an inability to act). We proactively manage hopelessness with Hope skills.

POSITIVE FEELINGS: Positive feelings are feelings that help us to stay Hopeful as we work towards our goals.

INSPIRED ACTIONS: Inspired actions are the deliberate steps you take toward your goals in life.

UPSTAIRS BRAIN: This is where our thinking, imagining, problem-solving, and learning occur. This part of the brain is responsible for the development of sound decision-making and planning, control over emotions and body, and self-understanding and empathy. The upstairs brain is also where we access our positive feelings.

DOWNSTAIRS BRAIN: Also referred to as the reptilian brain, this part of the brain is responsible for basic functions such as breathing, blinking, heart rate, fight, flight, freeze, and fawn mode. It is also responsible for the chemical stimuli associated with strong emotions, such as anger, sadness, and fear.

STRESS RESPONSE: Your stress response occurs when an external or internal trigger causes your brain to release stress hormones, such as cortisol, adrenaline, and norepinephrine, that force you into your fight, flight, freeze, or fawn mode.

STRESS SKILLS: These are actions that help you navigate your stress response and work through your body's chemical response to external stimuli.

HAPPINESS HABITS: These are healthy, long-term habits that help you stay in your upstairs brain, where you access the problem-solving skills, collaboration, and passion critical for Hope. When you take time for Happiness Habits, your brain releases happiness hormones, such as endorphins, dopamine, serotonin, and oxytocin.

NOURISHING NETWORKS: Your Nourishing Networks are made up of the people in your life who support you, help you stay on track, encourage you to succeed, and who you do the same for in return.

ELIMINATING CHALLENGES: Challenges to Hope are negative habits of thought, like limiting beliefs, automatic negative thoughts, all-or-nothing thinking, negative bias, rumination, worry, focusing on uncontrollables, and internalizing failure, that move us from Hope to hopelessness. Eliminating Challenges is the conscious act of using Hope skills to overcome these challenges to Hope and maintain Hopeful Mindsets™.

THE HOPE MATRIX™: The Hope Matrix is the process that we use to get from hopelessness to Hope, as well as the name of our podcast. The Hope Matrix teaches us that to cultivateHopeful Mindsets through our challenges, we must move from despair to positive feelings, and from helplessness to Inspired Actions.

SHINE HOPE™: This is the mnemonic we use to remember our Hope skills. SHINE stands for: **S**tress Skills, **H**appiness Habits, **I**nspired Actions, **N**ourishing Networks, and **E**liminating Challenges.

GROUP FACILITATION TIPS

Managing a group that allows everyone the opportunity to share while also keeping enough time for the facilitator to lead discussions requires a balance of encouragement, structure, and gentle redirection. Here are some practical tips:

1. Set Clear Guidelines at the Start: At the beginning of each session, let the group know how much time is available and how the session will be structured by walking them through the agenda for the day. Explain that everyone will have a chance to share, but for the sake of flow, time will need to be balanced between sharing and facilitator-led discussion.

2. Use a Time Limit for Sharing: Give each person a few minutes to speak. Consider using a timer or a visual cue, such as a subtle hand signal, to indicate when someone's time is nearly up. This helps prevent any one person from unintentionally dominating the conversation.

3. Encourage Brevity: Ask group members to focus on key points, encouraging them to share the most important thoughts rather than lengthy details. For example, say, "Let's each share one highlight or takeaway," to keep responses focused and concise.

4. Acknowledge and Redirect: When someone starts to veer off-topic or go too long, acknowledge their point and then gently steer back to the main discussion. Phrases like, "Thank you for sharing, that's really insightful. Let's come back to this topic as it ties into our next point…" work well for redirection without discouraging participation.

5. Incorporate Structured Group Rounds: Use a method where each person has a designated turn, one at a time, to briefly respond to a question or prompt. One option is to pass a "talking" object around that indicates whose turn it is to speak. This structure ensures that everyone knows they'll be able to share, while keeping responses succinct and organized.

6. Utilize Breakout or Partner Discussions: If you have a large group or limited time for the discussion questions, consider small breakout discussions or pairs. This allows more people to share with each other, while you, as the facilitator, stay on track with the main topics.

7. Use Reflective Summaries: Periodically summarize key points or themes from what members have shared. This shows you're listening and recognizes the value of each person's input while allowing you to steer the conversation toward the curriculum's objectives.

9. Create a "Parking Lot" for Off-Topic Points: Have a designated "parking lot" for tangential or in-depth topics that arise. These can be revisited later if time permits, but this strategy helps maintain the flow of the discussion.

10. Close with Group Reflection: Use the last few minutes of each session to encourage group members to share one takeaway or insight. This gives everyone a final chance to contribute meaningfully, while keeping the sesion organized and ensuring the facilitator can wrap up.

SETTING EXPECTATIONS FOR THE GROUP

Studies show that completing assignments between group sessions leads to better overall results[1]. To help group members gain a deeper understanding of the Five Keys to Shine framework, you'll assign a module from their workbook each week. This workbook will include a module that relates directly to the group discussion and provides additional information, along with thought-provoking prompts to solidify participants' learning.

1 https://link.springer.com/article/10.1007/s10608-010-9297-z

Hopeful Mindsets asks participants to be honest and vulnerable, and address many of their largest challenges and insecurities. It is therefore imperative that the peer group be a safe, supportive place to share and reflect.

Below, we have outlined some of the guidelines that you can share with group members to encourage positive peer group interactions.

STEPS TO EFFECTIVE LISTENING

Before beginning the modules, we encourage you to hold a preparation day to lay down group expectations and review skills to improve the cohesiveness among members. For example, the group can review **Dianne Shilling's 10 Steps to Effective Listening**[2]:

1. Face the speaker and maintain eye contact.
2. Be attentive, but relaxed.
3. Keep an open mind.
4. Listen to the speaker's words and try to picture what they're saying.
5. Don't interrupt and don't impose your "solutions."
6. Wait for the speaker to pause to ask clarifying questions.
7. Ask questions only to ensure understanding.
8. Try to feel what the speaker is feeling.
9. Give the speaker regular feedback.
10. Pay attention to what isn't said–to nonverbal cues.

Peer Sharing Guiding Principles:
- Be present
- Communicate freely
- Honor all opinions
- Critique ideas, not individuals
- Emphasize solutions
- Assume good intent/intentions
- Choose curiosity
- Ask for clarification
- Commit to the possibility of multiple (correct) points of view
- Share the airtime

2 https://www.forbes.com/sites/womensmedia/2012/11/09/10-steps-to-effective-listening/?sh=6d857e313891

Additional Guidelines for Peer Sharing:

BE AWARE OF OUTSIDER OVERCONFIDENCE: In the role of an outside peer, it can be easy to form impressions and judgments about another person's experiences. However, there are many things that outsiders do not know about a person or group's situation, interpersonal dynamics, or history.

SUPPORT: Offer empathy and understanding. Don't make assumptions (instead of saying "That's so frustrating!" or asking "Were you frustrated?", ask an open-ended question such as "What was that like for you?"). Think about what your peer might need at the moment.

IDEA-SHARING: Offer feedback with "intentional tentativeness" and curiosity rather than conclusiveness. This can reduce resistance and defensiveness and help the other person consider new possibilities.

- *"As you described that, I got the feeling that…Did you have that feeling too, or something else?"*
- *"I wonder what might have happened if you had…"*
- *Avoid "You should…I would…".*

IMPERFECTIONS: Exposing yourself to feedback from others creates vulnerability and runs the risk of revealing weaknesses, errors, or personal qualities that you may not want others to know. Permit yourself to be less than perfect. Be willing to allow others to recognize what you do well, and what you could do better. Be open to feedback and suggestions, and thank others for their support, insights, and constructive criticism.

SETTING GROUND RULES

Cover Key Areas: Make sure the following points are part of your ground rules:

- **Confidentiality:** Emphasize that what is shared in the group stays in the group, creating a safe space for open discussion.
- **Respectful Listening:** Encourage members to listen actively and avoid interrupting. Remind them that everyone's perspective is valuable, even if they disagree with what's said.
- **One Person Speaks at a Time:** This helps prevent confusion and ensures that everyone has a chance to be heard. If this becomes an issue throughout your sessions, try using a "talking piece" that indicates whose turn it is to speak.

- **Speak from Personal Experience:** Ask members to use "I" statements (like "I feel" or "In my experience"), which can help avoid generalizations and reduce defensiveness.
- **Time Awareness:** Remind everyone to be mindful of time when sharing so that everyone has a chance to speak within the allotted timeframe.
- **Be Supportive and Constructive:** Encourage group members to be positive and supportive, avoiding criticism or judgment.

ICEBREAKERS AND PRE-MODULE ACTIVITIES

Because of the nature of these peer group communications, there should be an intentional effort to give group members opportunities to get to know each other and get comfortable discussing a range of topics and interests. It may be helpful to hold these sessions outside (weather permitting) or in a less formalized space, to create a comfortable atmosphere for the group members. If you do stay inside, try to place chairs in a circle to allow all group members to see each other.

Possible Icebreaker topics:
- Small group activity where the group must find 3 common shared interests (sharing interests allows group members who have similar interests to connect if they want to)
- Small group activity where each person must find a unique hobby/interest that no one else in the group shares.
- Sharing what sparked their interest in taking a course on creating a Hopeful mindset.

Another alternative is to have the group do an activity together rather than have a conversation.

Examples:
- Keep a balloon in the air while passing it to each other in a circle.
- Create a "beat" together by one person making a sound (clapping) and the next person adding on a different sound (stomping) and so on.

MODULE 1: INTRODUCTION TO HOPE SCIENCE AND **SHINE HOPE™**

Module 1 is the first official meeting of the Hopeful Mindsets for Veterans group. Spend time going over module materials and discussing the purpose of the group. At the end of the module, group members should understand:

- The definition of Hope.
- The benefits of Hope.
- How to measure Hope.

SESSION PLAN

1. Welcome and Introduction (10 minutes)

- Greet participants and introduce yourself.
- Explain that the purpose of the program is to introduce Hope science and the Five Keys to Shine framework, which are the skills for growing Hope. Provide an overview of the structure of the sessions.

2. Icebreaker Activity (15 minutes)

- Choose an icebreaker activity from the activities described in the Facilitation Tips to begin building rapport among group members.

3. Discussion: What is Hope? (10 minutes)

- Share The Hope Matrix visual, and our Hope definition that includes both feelings and actions: Define Hope using the workbook definition: "Hope is a vision for the future, fueled by both positive feelings and inspired actions."
- Reiterate that Hope is different from a wish or optimism because Hope requires action.
- **Discuss:** Hope is like a muscle; it must be developed and strengthened. People who face lots of challenges must work on building their 'Hope muscle' more than others, just like people working to overcome a physical injury. Hope can be learned at any age. Ask for everyone's perspective on this. Reinforce the Science of Hope and how Hope is a measurable, teachable, and learnable skill. Pay special attention to the Five Keys to Shine Hope, as these will be reaffirmed throughout the course and are how we teach all to grow and strengthen the Hope muscle.

4. Module Activity (15 minutes)

As a group (or in smaller groups depending on the size of the group), discuss:

- Each person will share their definition of Hope. (Make sure they include both feelings and action - Hope is more than a wish)
- As a group, come to a consensus on a definition of Hope and share the new definition of Hope for your group on the whiteboard.
- Talk as a group about what you are Hopeful for in life, and how what you Hope for in life relates to this new definition of Hope that includes both positive feelings and inspired actions.

5. Module Debrief (10 minutes)

Go over the whiteboard as a group and discuss each group's definition. Have each group discuss why Hope is important to them based on this new definition, how it impacts their life, and how learning Hope can benefit others around them.

Wrap-up and Homework

- Summarize key takeaways from the session that Hope is teachable and learnable at any age.
- Share the Hope Scale, workbook, and ask all to complete Module One prior to the next session.
- If you'd like to, pair everyone up to form 'accountability partners' for daily check-ins during the week. You can share that we are up to 95% more likely to achieve a goal if we write it down, and check-in with someone about it regularly. Daily check-ins can be as simple as a daily text or phone call to one another.

MODULE 2: ANTITHESIS OF HOPE: HOPELESSNESS

Module 2 focuses on hopelessness as the antithesis of Hope. It is sometimes easier to understand what something is (i.e. Hope) once we know what it isn't (Hopelessness). At the end of the module, group members should understand:

- The definition of hopelessness, and how it has both emotional and motivational components.
- The impact of hopelessness on various areas of their lives.
- Why hopelessness is likely higher for veterans, and why it is extra important that they understand 'how' to Hope.

SESSION PLAN

1. Welcome (15 minutes)

- Recap the previous session.
- Ask all participants to share their feelings about their Hope score. They don't have to share their actual score, as it is a personal unit of measurement. The lower their score, the more the individual needs to practice their Hope skills.
- Ask group members to briefly share (1) their top strength from the VIA and how it shows up in their day-to-day life, and (2) their "why" for participating in the group.

2. Discussion (10 minutes)

- Define hopelessness as emotional despair and motivational helplessness.
- Normalize that everyone experiences moments of hopelessness and explain that left unresolved, these can turn into persistent hopelessness.
- **Discuss** specific outcomes related to unresolved hopelessness for veterans, such as -
  - Hopelessness is strongly linked to the emergence and severity of PTSD symptoms (Chang et al., 2016; Scher & Resick, 2005).
  - Hopelessness partially explains the relationship between nightmares and suicidal behaviors in trauma victims (Littlewood et al., 2016).
  - Disabled veterans, veterans above 40, and those who had active services in the military have the highest levels of hopelessness among veterans (Karatas et al., 2019).

3. Module Activity (20 minutes)

As a group (or in smaller groups depending on the size of the group), complete the following parts.

- **Part 1:** Come up with a list of moments in which participants have experienced hopelessness. Identify the aspects of emotional despair and motivational helplessness in each moment. This should take approximately 5-10 mins.
- **Part 2** *(if group members were split into smaller groups):* Have the small groups call out the emotional indicators of hopelessness to the entire group and write them on the whiteboard, looking for overlap. Repeat this process for the motivational indicators.
- **Part 3:** Return to small groups to finish discussing how identifying the feelings and actions can help to bring awareness to being in a state of hopelessness. Next, discuss actions or best practices that you can take to help yourself get out of these moments.

4. My Shine Hope Story Review and Module Wrap Up (10 minutes)

Introduce My Hope Story as an ongoing narrative the group members will add to as they learn skills in each module to help solidify their understanding of the Shine Hope Framework. Explain that they will write about either:

- A current challenge they are struggling to overcome (this way the group can help generate ideas to overcome the challenge)
- A past challenge they have overcome (this lets them remember a challenge and the skills they used to get through it which they can then pull to work through future challenges)
- A person in their life, a celebrity, or a leader who has faced a similar challenge to something they are experiencing and can provide valuable insights. They can identify the skills that person used to overcome the same challenge by interviewing the person or researching them online and finding any interviews they've shared
- Explain that this week, participants will identify what they want to write their 'My Shine Hope Story' about. It doesn't have to be a big challenge, it can be something smaller to ease into the process. Participants should choose something that they're willing to talk about with the group. Everyone will be discussing their stories weekly and brainstorming ideas together.

- You can view other Veteran Shine Hope Stories here, or listen to The Hope Matrix Podcasts with episodes from a few Veterans to learn more.
  - **Finding Hope After Active Military Duty, Featuring MaCherie Dunbar:** www.theHopematrix.com/2024/07/05/finding-Hope-after-active-military-duty-featuring-macherie-dunbar/
  - **Being Intentional In Navigating Hope As A Veteran, Featuring Thomas Harris:** www.theHopematrix.com/2024/07/05/being-intentional-in-navigating-Hope-as-a-veteran-and-civilian-featuring-thomas-harris/
- One of the biggest challenges veterans face is going from active duty to civilian life, so this may be something you want to encourage them to write about. The idea is to be proactive and creative about how to solve the challenges we face

5. Review and Wrap up

- Summarize key takeaways from the session: moments of hopelessness are normal, and we can use the Five Keys to Shine to proactively manage hopelessness and find our way back to Hope.
- Ensure all know how to find the Shine Hope Story, and have them write about their chosen challenge, identifying both the despair and feelings of helplessness in the first paragraph, as well as including a picture.
- Ensure all have a check-in partner (new, if desired) to keep on track. Assign the workbook exercises related to Module Two for the next session.

MODULE 3: STRESS SKILLS

Module 3 focuses on identifying and practicing Stress Skills to move away from the emotional despair associated with hopelessness. At the end of the module, group members should:

- Recognize the impact of stress on Hope.
- Understand the difference between the "upstairs brain" and "downstairs brain".
- Understand the importance of the 90-second pause and deep belly breathing.
- Have a working list of Stress Skills they can begin practicing.

SESSION PLAN

1. Welcome (10 minutes)

- Recap the previous session.
- Ask the group to share the challenge they are writing about during the course or why learning to proactively manage hopelessness is important to them.
- Ask someone to share their intro paragraph to their Shine Hope Story.

2. Discussion (10 minutes)

Explain the stress response and the 90-second pause:

- The 90-second rule says that when you are triggered by something in your environment, a chemical process takes place in your body for approximately 90 seconds. For 90 seconds after the environmental trigger, your body is flooded with stress hormones, such as cortisol, adrenaline, and norepinephrine.
- You are unable to access your critical thinking and problem-solving skills when you are actively triggered. Often, we can make VERY BAD decisions such as resorting to violence, addiction, and self-harm. That is why it's important to learn how to make it through the 90 seconds following a trigger.
- **Discuss:** Look at the Trigger Worksheet in the workbook, and start talking about common triggers the group has. **Ask the group to brainstorm** how they can get through the 90 seconds when triggered so they don't react. Write options on the whiteboard.

3. Deep Breathing Activity (5 minutes)

Deep belly breathing slows heart rate and blood pressure, which are often heightened during a stress response. Encourage group members to practice deep breathing together using the following prompts:

- Sit in a comfortable position with your back as straight as possible.
- Notice how your body feels. Take a few seconds to just relax. Relax your neck, shoulders, arms, legs, and feet. Can you feel your heartbeat? Can you sense your breath? Try a few big inhales and exhales.
- When you're ready, place one hand on your chest and the other on your belly button (below the rib cage).
- Now, take a long, slow, deep breath in through your nose for a count of 10 (or as long as you are able). As you breathe in, you want to send the air to your belly button. Your hand on your belly should rise while the hand on your chest remains still.
- Once you get to 10, slowly exhale out of your mouth. Feel the muscles of your stomach tighten and your hand lower.
- Do this for at least 90 seconds (or 10 slow, deep breaths).

4. Module Activity (20 minutes)

As a group (or in smaller groups depending on the size of the group), complete the following parts.

- **Part 1:** Identify the physiological response to stressors and the Stress Skills that you can employ to help reduce your stress symptoms.
- **Part 2:** Review the worksheet with both positive and negative ways to get Stress Hormones and the Allostatic slope that shows the optimal amounts of hormones needed. Discuss unhealthy things we may be doing, and healthier choices we can make.
- **Part 3:** Return to small groups and share best practices and how participants can use these skills going forward.

5. My Hope Story Review and Wrap up

- Summarize key takeaways from the session.
- Explain that this week, group members will write about the Stress Skills for their My Shine Hope Story. Participants should be very specific about the Stress Skills needed to get through the challenge.
- Assign the workbook exercises related to module three for the next session, and have everyone get a new check-in partner if desired.
- Ask participants to notice which Stress Skills they use throughout the week and intentionally practice at least one before the next session.

MODULE 4: HAPPINESS HABITS

Module 4 explains that Happiness Habits are long-term actions that are intended to foster healthy, positive feelings that help you stay in your upstairs brain. At the end of the module, group members should:

- Explain how positive feelings relate to Hope and how staying in your upstairs brain keeps your mindset primed for Hope.
- Recognize the importance of gratitude as a Happiness Habit.
- Generate a list of Happiness Habits to start practicing regularly.

SESSION PLAN

1. Welcome (10 minutes)

- Recap previous session.
- Ask group members to briefly share a Stress Skill they practiced and what they noticed when they practiced it.
- Ask someone to share their Stress Skill portion of their My Shine Hope Story.

2. Discussion (10 minutes)

- Explain that Happiness Habits are the second Key to Shine Hope and that they are long-term actions that cause the brain to release happy hormones (i.e., endorphins, dopamine, serotonin, and oxytocin).
- Happiness Habits help us stay in the upstairs brain and should be practiced every day as they help combat the negative impacts of stress and excess stress hormones.
- Give examples of Happiness Habits from the workbook.

3. Gratitude Exercise (15 minutes)

Explain that gratitude is an example of a Happiness Habit that the group will practice today. This exercise is taken from Dr. Dan Tomasulo's, *Learned Hopefulness* book.

- **Part 1:** Ask the group to spend 3 minutes writing down everything that happened in their life yesterday. Instruct them to focus on their thoughts and feelings during the reflection.

- **Part 2:** Ask the group to take another 3 minutes to write down everything that happened to them yesterday, but instead, frame it through the lens of gratitude. What or who were they grateful for during their day?
- **Part 3:** Discuss the difference between the two exercises with the group. Which day was better? How did you feel when writing each? What else did you notice? Gratitude is an intentional practice. It releases endorphins and is good for us, but it isn't necessarily natural.

4. Module Activity (15 minutes)

As a group (or in smaller groups depending on the size of the group), complete the following parts.
- **Part 1:** Have group members make a collaborative list of current Happiness Habits they employ and how these habits make them feel. Be sure to think about what Happiness Habits they practiced when they were kids. We often stop doing what makes us happy as adults, and it can be useful to return to what brought us joy as children.
- **Part 2:** Discuss the lists that each group has come up with. Write Happiness Habits that overlap between groups on the whiteboard and discuss commonalities.
- **Part 3:** Return to small groups, discuss how you feel after completing your Happiness Habit, what other new habits you learned about, and why you'd like to try them.

5. My Shine Hope Story Review and Wrap Up (5 minutes)

- Explain that this week, the group members will write about the Happiness Habits related to their My Shine Hope Story. Remind them to be as specific, and to provide as many Happiness Habits as possible. Make sure participants identify healthy habits!
- Summarize key takeaways from the session.
- Encourage participants to notice the Happiness Habits they use throughout the coming week and to intentionally practice at least one.
- Assign the workbook exercises related to Module Four for the next session, and have everyone get a new check-in partner if desired.

MODULE 5: INSPIRED ACTIONS

Module 5 is about the Third Key to Shine Hope and covers a variety of goal-setting techniques that allow us to proactively move from hopelessness toward what we want in life. At the end of the module, the group members should understand:

- The difference between achievement and avoidance goals.
- The difference between intrinsic and extrinsic goals.
- The WOOP and SMART goal frameworks.
- Stretch goals and micro goals.
- Regoaling.

SESSION PLAN

1. Welcome (10 minutes)
- Recap the previous session.
- Ask group members to share the Happiness Habit(s) they practiced over the week and what they noticed when they practiced it.

2. Discussion (15 minutes)
Explain how to brainstorm goals using the WOOP framework:
- **WISH:** Think about what you want in life. Pick a wish that is challenging but that you can still fulfill.
- **OUTCOME:** What would be the best possible outcome if your wish came true? How would fulfilled your wish make you feel?
- **OBSTACLE:** What is within you or in your environment that keeps you from fulfilling your wish?
- **PLAN:** Identify one action you can take or thought you can think of to overcome your obstacle. Then, make an if-then plan: IF (I encounter this obstacle) THEN (I will use this solution).

Explain SMART goals, and how stretch goals and micro-goals should be included:
- **SMART Goals:** Goals that are Specific, Measurable, Attainable, Relevant, and Time-bound. Refer to the SMART Goals poster for more information.

3. Module Activity (20 minutes)
As a group (or in smaller groups depending on the size of the group), complete the following parts.
- **Part 1:** Have group members share their individual WOOP Goals and discuss the actions they can take to overcome their obstacles.

- **Part 2:** Have group members share their individual SMART Goals and discuss the actions they can take to achieve these goals with a focus on how they keep their goals measurable. Plan what obstacles may arise and how group members can overcome the obstacles.
- **Part 3:** <u>Discuss</u> areas of life they want to set goals in right now. List the top 3 areas they want to improve, then focus on one goal at a time, breaking it down into steps (chunking). Explain that if we try to tackle too many goals at once, it can become overwhelming, so it's best to make progress through manageable steps.
- **Part 4:** <u>Discuss</u> regoaling. It is easy to stay in persistent hopelessness when we need to regoal, but are hanging on to a goal or plan of action that is not currently attainable for us. Learning how regoaling relates to maintaining our Hope is a critical part of understanding the Shine Hope Framework.

At this point, you can share our founder's story with the group as an example of the power of regoaling. The founder of the Shine Hope Company lost her dad to suicide. She desperately wanted him to be alive, and was stuck in a state of hopelessness (sadness, anger, fear, and helplessness) because her goal was not attainable. She eventually tried to take her own life. She learned had no choice but to 'regoal', recognizing that her goal to have her dad back in her life was not a SMART goal because it was not attainable.

At this point, she redirected her energy to find 'father-like' mentors in her life, which led her to meet Dr. Myron Belfer, a Harvard Catalyst who helped her create this very program. This process of regoaling helped her focus on what was in her control and develop healthy coping strategies for her grief.

4. My Hope Story Review and Wrap Up (5 minutes)
- Explain that this week, the group members should focus on Inspired Actions related to their My Shine Hope Story, identifying steps to address their chosen challenge. Encourage them to get as specific as possible in their description!
- Summarize key takeaways from the session.
- Assign the workbook exercises related to Module Six for the next session, and have everyone get a new check-in partner if desired.
- Encourage participants to brainstorm one SMART goal they'd like to start working toward or are already working to achieve and how they are going to get there.

MODULE 6: NOURISHING NETWORKS

Module 6 focuses on the importance of having a network for Hope and asks group members to try and visualize what an actual network for Hope may look like. After the module, group members should understand:

- The importance of a Nourishing Network in moving toward Hope.
- How to identify people in their lives that fit into their Nourishing Network.
- Methods to Strengthen their Nourishing Network and to identify people in their life that are not 'nourishing'. Remember, you are most like the people you surround yourself with, so be sure to reflect on whether they are healthy for you.
- **Important:** Ensure that every group member can identify at least one person they can turn to in a time of need. If someone cannot identify a single person, work with them to find a person or offer to be that person, if you feel able. Every group member must have at least one identified person they can turn to.

SESSION PLAN

1. Welcome (10 minutes)
- Recap the previous session.
- Ask group members to briefly share the SMART goal they are working toward and how they plan to meet their first micro goal. Ask the group members to share an obstacle that may arise while working towards their SMART goal and have the group brainstorm strategies for overcoming the obstacle. Explain that planning for obstacles that may arise before they even come up is a great step to proactively protect your hopeful mindset.

2. Discussion (15 minutes)
Review what a Nourishing Network is and emphasize that people in the network should include:
- People who know and understand you
- People who value your strengths
- People who help you activate the Shine framework
- People whom you trust and can confide in
- People who are available to support you
- People you are willing to do the above for as well

- Point out that we are 95% more likely to achieve goals if we write them down and check in with someone regularly about them.
- Provide examples of people who could be part of a Nourishing Network, such as doctors, therapists, or other medical professionals, family/friends, spiritual leaders, or even pets.

3. Strengthening your Hope Network (10 minutes)

- Note that one can strengthen their relationships through empathy, praise, recognition, kindness, compassion, strong communication, gratitude, and the 5:1 rule (for every negative or constructive criticism you say to someone, say five positive things).
- Invite group members to write down five things they love about one person in their Nourishing Network and encourage them to share the five positive things with that person.
  - If someone cannot identify a person in their Nourishing Network, work with them individually to figure out a person they can add.

4. Module Activity (20 minutes)

As a group (or in smaller groups depending on the size of the group), complete the following parts.

- **Part 1:** Have group members make a list of the qualities they want to have in their Nourishing Network.
- **Part 2: Discuss** ways to improve your Hope network. You may want to do this as it relates to a specific goal: getting healthier, playing sports, ending an addiction, finding a relationship, school, getting a job, etc. How can we create better, healthier networks? Brainstorm ways to make new connections.
- **Part 3: Discuss** gratitude and practice kindness in action. Spend time having everyone recognize at least one person (and make sure everyone is recognized) with something specific related to how they have positively impacted their life. Be as specific as possible—specificity is key to fostering gratitude. "I'm grateful that you shared with me how I might overcome my obstacle last week when I shared my Shine Hope Story" will be more effective than "I'm grateful for you."

- **Part 4: (Optional Activity)** Grab a ball of yarn that you will pass around the entire group. Beginning with the instructor, mention a quality that you look for in your network of Hope. Have someone from the group who has this quality raise their hand and pass the ball of yarn to them, with the original person still holding the starting piece of yarn. This will continue with each person who has the ball of yarn stating a quality from their list that they look for in their network of Hope, each time someone raises their hand to identify they have this quality, the yarn ball is passed, and a spiderweb/network of string eventually connects everyone multiple times through multiple axis.
- This activity identifies group members who could be potential parts of each member's Nourishing Network.

5. My Hope Story Review and Wrap Up (5 Minutes)
- Explain that this week, the group members will write about their Nourishing Network in their My Shine Hope Story.
- Make sure everyone has access to the resources page, and knows where to go if they need support. Everyone needs at least one person they can count on.
- Summarize key takeaways from the session.
- Assign the workbook exercises related to Module Seven for the next session, and have everyone get a new check-in partner if desired.

MODULE 7: ELIMINATING CHALLENGES

Module 7 focuses on the idea behind eliminating challenges to Hope and why it is important. By the end of the module, group members should:

- Recognize how negative thought patterns lead to hopelessness.
- Learn how to counteract challenges with Shine Hope skills.

SESSION PLAN

1. Welcome (10 minutes)

- Recap the previous session.
- Ask group members to share one person in their Nourishing Network and how they support them in reaching a goal or navigating current obstacles in life.

2. Discussion (25 minutes)

Review the unhelpful thought patterns that can lead to persistent hopelessness and how to overcome them.

- **Limiting Beliefs:** Limiting beliefs are negative thoughts or opinions that we tell ourselves are true that keep us in a negative mindset. They are at the core of our anxieties, fears, and insecurities. To truly create, maintain, and grow Hope, we must first identify the limiting beliefs we have around Hope and find ways to overcome them.
- **Automatic Negative Thoughts:** Automatic negative thoughts (ANTs) are repetitive negative thoughts that we form instantaneously in response to external stimuli. They're often hurtful or irrational and can send us into a spiral of hopelessness if not managed.
- **All-or-Nothing Thinking:** All-or-nothing thinking is a negative thought pattern in which we only think in extremes. Rather than seeing all of the solutions to a problem, all-or-nothing thinking forces us to only see either complete success or complete failure.
- **Negative Bias:** Negativity bias refers to the psychological phenomenon that causes negative events to have a greater impact on our brains than positive ones. We tend to fixate on criticism rather than compliments, pay more attention to bad news than good news, and notice negative events happening near us instead of positive ones. Negativity bias forces us into our downstairs brain and can have lasting impacts on our relationships, behavior, and Hope.

- **Rumination:** Rumination refers to when we repeatedly go over a thought or a problem from the past in our heads, without end. Rumination is associated with numerous negative mental states, including depression, anxiety, post-traumatic stress disorder, and hopelessness.
- **Worry:** Worry is when we feel anxious or afraid about real or imagined future scenarios. Where rumination focuses on the past, worry focuses on the future. Worry forces us to fixate on and respond to future dangers that we think we may encounter.
- **Focusing on Uncontrollables:** Focusing on Uncontrollables is when you focus on things that are outside of your power or influence. This can lead to rumination and worry, which can in turn cause stress, anxiety, and depression. It is important to proactively manage what you can control and learn to release what you cannot.
- **Attaching to Outcomes:** Attaching to outcomes is when we set goals, and are then unable or unwilling to be satisfied unless we reach that specific goal. While goal setting is important, it is also important to have a sense of active surrender and know that sometimes there is a better path to our goals. Being too attached to specific goal attainment leads to hopelessness when we don't reach that goal.
- **Internalizing Failure:** There is a biological link between failure and our physical and mental health. When we achieve our goals, our brains release testosterone and dopamine, and we experience positive feelings. Science has found that, with time and repetition, these chemicals can alter the chemistry of our brains positively. The opposite is also true. If we fail early while others succeed and internalize that failure instead of learning from it, we are more likely to make future mistakes and have lowered future confidence.

3. Module Activity (15 minutes)

As a group (or in smaller groups depending on the size of the group), complete the following parts.

- **Part 1:** Have group members write down their three biggest challenges. Then have them write down how they may Eliminate Challenges now that they've learned more ways to do so.
- **Part 2:** Have group members take a specific challenge they've identified and discuss ways to navigate it. Brainstorm things like Stress Skills and Happiness Habits to stop challenges like rumination, internalizing failure, and worrying about the future. Allow time for group members to resonate and respond to each other. As the facilitator, try to create common ties between the different examples that are given, and expand on responses.

- **Part 3:** <u>Discuss</u> one common specific problem someone is facing (i.e. finding a job, addiction, health). On a board, draw a circle. Inside the circle, put the things that can be controlled about the situation. Outside the circle, put the things that can not be controlled about the situation. Be as creative as possible.

4. My Hope Story Review and Wrap Up

- Explain that this week, the group members will write about using the skills learned in the Eliminating Challenges module to overcome the challenge they are writing about, whether that means identifying what skills they can use when facing their current challenge, the skills they used in a past challenge, or the skills the person they are writing about used.
- Summarize key takeaways from the session; planning how to Eliminate Challenges before they arise helps reduce the likelihood of hopelessness and provides proactive strategies for moving toward goals.
- Assign the workbook exercises related to module eight for the next session.
- **Ask group members to remeasure their Hope using the Hope scale in their workbook before the next module.**

MODULE 8: BUILDING A VISION FOR HOPE

Module 8 is the final module of the program and will serve as a debriefing and wrap-up session.

SESSION PLAN

1. Welcome (20 minutes)

- Recap the previous session.
- Ask group members to briefly share when they noticed a negative thinking pattern in the last week and what they did when they noticed it.
- **Give group members 10 minutes to remeasure their Hope score and complete the post course feedback survey (or you can leave time at end)**
  - **Hope Scale:** www.theshinehopecompany.com/veterans-resources/
  - **Post-Course Survey:** https://form.jotform.com/241990879649479

Veterans Hope Scale   **Post-Course Survey**

2. Discussion (5 minutes)

- Review the Shine framework: Stress Skills, Happiness Habits, Inspired Actions, Nourishing Networks, and Eliminating Challenges.
- Note that these skills need to be continuously practiced to continue growing Hope.
- Emphasize that now that participants know these skills, it can be helpful to teach others the framework to solidify their learning and share knowledge with others who have not been taught how to Hope or how to manage hopelessness.

3. Module Activity (20 minutes)

- **Option 1:** In this activity, group members will be doing a "speed dating" style discussion. To do this, break group members up into two lines with an equal number of people. When the timer starts, each group member takes turns sharing their Hope story with their partner. Depending on the size of the group, you may want to allow anywhere between two to four minutes per pair. After the time has elapsed, have one of the lines move to their left, with the person at the end moving to the opposite end, so that everyone has a new partner. Do this until the moving line is back in its original position.

- **Option 2:** Have everyone read their own My Shine Hope Story, or give them to the person next to them to have another person read their My Shine Hope Story. Allow time for participants to give feedback on the story they read and have each person share what they liked most about it, what they learned from it, or how it inspired them.

4. Group Discussion (10 minutes)
- Ask group members to reflect on what they thought this group was going to be versus what they experienced.
- Ask them to share their biggest takeaway from the course and what they will remember the most/use the most moving forward.
- Ask them to reflect on the change in their Hope score throughout the group and what positively or negatively impacted their score.
- Ask group members to reflect on how they will inspire Hope in the lives of those around them.

5. Resources (5 minutes)
- Remind the group of the list of resources group members can turn to if they need future support or services. Encourage them to use it proactively; we don't want to wait until a time of crisis to get support.
- Remind the group that as veterans, they are likely going to experience more moments of hopelessness than most. Because of this, they must strengthen their Hope muscle and give more attention to Hope than others. The more obstacles we face, the more we need to Shine Hope.
- Encourage group members to take the post-course survey, it helps us improve our program for others. We increase Hope scores for everyone if we find better ways to share our work. Thank participants for helping us make this a success.
- Encourage group members to teach Hope skills to kids. Our kids are experiencing unprecedented rates of hopelessness, and the best way to create strong skills around Hope is by teaching it. All of our programs are scripted, so anyone can teach them anywhere kids gather (school, after-school programs, places of worship, clubs, etc.). Find out more about teaching Hope at www.Hopefulminds.org.

Veterans Resources:
www.theshinehopecompany.com/veterans-resources/